GET MOVING!

ACTION RHYMES AND POEMS TO READ ALOUD
WRITTEN AND ILLUSTRATED BY

KEV PAYNE

For all the schools I've had the pleasure of visiting, all the children I've had the joy of working with and all the team at Authors Abroad - KP

Text and Illustrations by
Kev Payne

ISBN 978-1-9196148-6-1

First Published in 2023
by Caboodle Books

Printed and manufactured in the UK
Copyright © 2023 Kev Payne. All Rights Reserved.
No part of this book (visual or textual) may be used or reproduced in any manner whatsoever without written permission, by the authors or publisher, except in the case of quotations embodied in critical articles and reviews. Permission for the use of sources, graphics, illustrations, and text copy are solely permitted by the creators of this book.

www.kevpayne.com

Caboodle Books Limited, Riversdale, Rivock Avenue,
Keighley, West Yorkshire, BD20 6SA

CONTENTS

Poems...4

Story Stew...5

Music Makers..6

Sweeties..7

Get Moving!..8

Football...10

The Wind...11

Ready to Race...12

Wake Up Wiggle..14

Dragon...15

Hello, Little Firework...16

I Like to Dance..17

Super Sloth...18

Have You Seen My Friend?..20

'I like' Rap...21

Dinotastic..22

Let's Play!..24

This is NOT a circle..25

Cucumbers..26

Animal Talk...27

Have a Great Day!...28

Anywhere..29

Poems

With poems you get to play with words
It feels like you can pick up a dictionary
Shake all the words out onto the table
Scoop them up with your hands
Let them dribble through your fingers
You can mash them
Scrunch them
Mould them
Pack them tight like snow and build amazing shapes
Or you can stretch them
Snip them
Clip them
Pinch them
Throw them in the air and let them rain down like confetti
And with all this
Snipping
Squashing
Shaking and jumbling
Poems will start to appear
Some people like them to rhyme
Some people like them in neat little rows
Some people like them with rules
Some people like them to fly free as a bird
But me
I like them all
For poems can make you laugh
Make you cry
Make you think
Inspire and delight you
Stir and ignite you
Each has a rhythm, a heartbeat, a soul
The poems are waiting
Are you ready to play?

Story Stew

Start with a witch
Drop in a knight
Chuck in a dragon
Stir in a fight
Plop in an alien
Drizzle in drama
A sprinkle of magic
A dash of llama
Mix in pirates
A pinch of laughter
Spoon in treasure
Add a happy ever after
Let it simmer
Stir the pot
Not too cold
Not too hot
Mix it well
Lick the spoon
Our story will be ready soon

Music Makers

We are music makers
We can play the drum!
Boom! Boom! Music makers
We are having fun

We are music makers
The trumpet we can play!
Toot! Toot! Music makers
We are on our way

We are music makers
We can play guitar!
Twang! Twang! Music makers
We are superstars!

We are music makers
We can play as one!
Boom! Toot! Twang! Toot! Twang! Boom!
What a lot of fun!

Sweeties

1, 2
Chew, chew
3, 4
Give me more!
5, 6
Pick and mix
7, 8
These are great!
9, 10
Start again!

Get Moving!

Stretch, stretch
Blink, blink
Shake, shake
Wink, wink
Wriggle, wriggle, wriggle and jump
Get moving!
Wriggle, wriggle, wriggle and jump
Get moving!

Tip, tip
Tap, tap
Nod, nod
Clap, clap
Wriggle, wriggle, wriggle and jump
Get moving!
Wriggle, wriggle, wriggle and jump
Get moving!

High, high
Low, low
Fast, fast
Slow, slow
Wriggle, wriggle, wriggle and jump
Get moving!
Wriggle, wriggle, wriggle and jump
Get moving!

Left, left
Right, right
Shhh! Shhh!
Night, night

Football

We can kick it

We can flick it

We can shoot it in the goal

We can chip it

We can cross it

We can punt it with our toe

We can lob it

We can chop it

We can pass it to a friend

We can clear it

We can strike it

We can curl it with some bend

We can head it

We can hook it

We can swerve it round the wall

Dribble, volley, smash it

We just love football!

The Wind

Sometimes the wind can be soft

It tickles the trees

Ruffles my hair

And pushes my sailboat down the river

Sometimes the wind can be hard

It whips the leaves

Pinches my neck

And pushes me back indoors

I like it best when

It whispers

Cools my face

And helps my kite to dance

READY TO RACE

Let's get ready,
Ready to race,
I'm wearing my kit,
Got a smile on my face,
Let's get ready, ready to run,
And I know that we will have some fun,

I can run, run, run,
I can jog, jog, jog,
I can leap in the air like a jumpy frog,
I want to be a winner but no matter the prize,
I feel great when I exercise,

Let's get ready,
Ready to race,
I'm wearing my kit,
Got a smile on my face,
Let's get ready, ready to run,
And I know that we will have some fun,

I can jump, jump, jump,
I can bound, bound, bound,
I can wiggle and wriggle like a bug on the ground,
I want to be a winner but if I'm not number 1,
I know that you and me will have some fun,

Let's get ready,
Ready to race,
I'm wearing my kit,
Got a smile on my face,
Let's get ready, ready to run,
And I know that we will have some fun,

I can hop, hop, hop,
I can ski, ski, ski,
I can dive in the water like a fish in the sea,
I want to be a winner and if I really try,
I know that I will feel great inside,

Let's get ready,
Ready to race,
I'm wearing my kit,
Got a smile on my face,
Let's get ready, ready to run,
On your marks, get set...

GO!

Wake Up Wiggle

When I wake up in the morning

I give myself a giggle

I get my body moving with the wake up wiggle

I wiggle my fingers

I wiggle my nose

I wiggle my shoulders

I wiggle my toes

I wiggle my elbows

I wiggle my thighs

I wiggle my bottom

I wiggle my eyes

I wiggle my ankles

I wiggle my tongue

I wiggle my whole body

Then my wiggling is done!

Dragon

Dragon swish

Dragon swoop

Dragon fly a loop-the-loop

Dragon claw

Dragon bite

Dragon fire light up the night

Dragon snarl

Dragon roar

Dragon tired now

Dragon snore

Hello, Little Firework

Hello, little firework
How high will you go?
Show me all your colours
Help the sky to glow

Farewell, little firework
Light the world below
Thank you, little firework
You put on quite a show

I love to dance

When I feel my body slumping
I know what will get me jumping
So I get the music thumping
I get my heart pumping

1, 2, 3!

I love to dance
I love to spring
I love to boogie
I love to swing
I love to tango
I love to prance
I love to rumba
I love to dance

Jazz, Ballet, Hip Hop, Samba,
Mambo, Quickstep, Robot, Salsa,
Tap, Cha Cha, Charleston, Jive
Dancing makes me feel alive!

1, 2, 3!
I love to dance
I love to dance
I love to dance

Super Sloth!

Who flies high up in the sky?
Who makes all the villains cry?
Who speaks up for those who are shy?
Super sloth! That super guy!

Who lifts cars and boats and planes?
Who can stop fast-moving trains?
Who has brawn but also brains?
Super sloth! That super guy!

Who has strength as well as speed?
Who will come when you're in need?
If you are trapped who'll get you freed?
Super sloth! That super guy!

Who will always do their best?
Who will always pass the test?
Who's super tired and needs a rest?
Super sloth! That super guy!

Who is yawning in the trees?
Whose eyes are closing in the breeze?
Whose snores are rustling the leaves?
Super sloth! That super guy!
Super sloth! That super guy!

Have you seen my friend?

Her ears are soft

Her tongue is tickly

Her feet are tiny

Her back is prickly

Her footsteps are gentle

Her eyes are bright

She sleeps in the day and comes out at night

Have you seen my friend? Well if you do…

Give her a wave and say 'Yoo hoo!'

'I LIKE' RAP

I like chocolate, ice cream, snacks and sweets

I like birthdays, parties, games and treats

I like yellow, green, pink and blue

But most of all I like you!

Ready, steady, pass the mic

Come on everybody tell us what you like

Ready, steady, pass the mic

Come on everybody tell us what you like

I like pizza, spaghetti, chips and cakes

I like monkeys, lions, dogs and snakes

I like days at the park and trips to the zoo

But most of all I like you!

Ready, steady, pass the mic

Come on everybody tell us what you like

Ready, steady, pass the mic

These are the things we like

Dinotastic!

Dinobig
Dinosmall
Dinoshort
Dinotall
Dinoup
Dinodown
Dinosmile
Dinofrown
Dinohot
Dinocold
Dinoyoung
Dinoold
Dinohappy
Dinosad
Dinogood
Dinobad
Dinohigh
Dinolow
Dinofast
Dinoslow
Dinoshallow
Dinodeep
Dinowake
Dinosleep
Dinowhispers
Dinoroars
Dinotastic Dinosaurs!

23

Let's Play

Let's play dinosaurs

Roar! Roar! Stomp!

Let's play elephants

Thud! Thump! Clomp!

Let play seals

Arf! Arf! Clap!

Let's play crocodiles

Ready, steady, snap!

Let's play rockets

Zip! Zap! Zoom!

Let's play fireworks

Sizzle! Crack! Boom!

Let's play robots

Click! Whirr! Zip!

Let's play hairdressers

Trim! Brush! Snip!

Let's play

Let's play

What do you want to play today?

This is ~~a~~ **NOT** circle

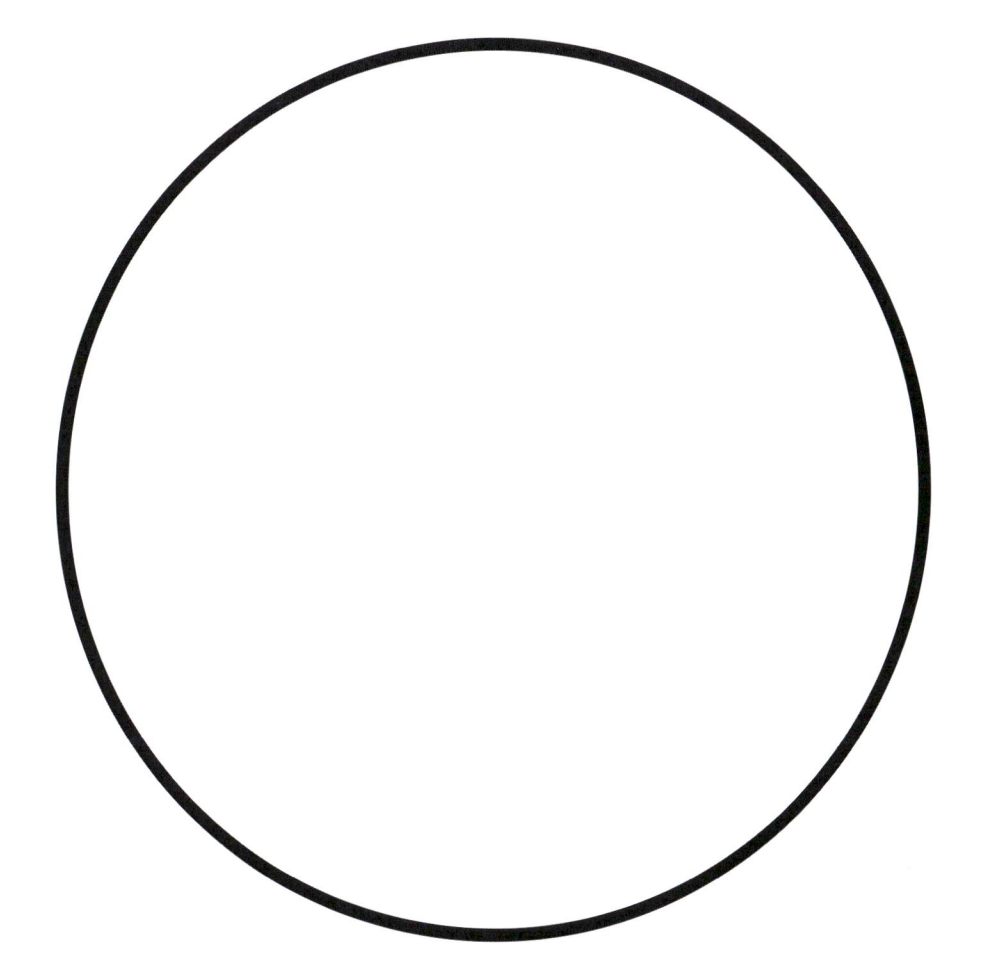

This is...

a clown's nose waiting to be honked

a silent moon above chattering stars

a flaming hoop ready for a stuntman

a big, red button that shouldn't be pressed

a football placed on the penalty spot

a stolen coin at the bottom of the sea

a gooey pizza smothered in bubbling cheese

a dragon's eye staring out from a cave

The Earth - brilliant, bright and brimming with possibilities

Cucumbers!

Welcome to fun foods!
We've got…
Cucumbers!
Boocumbers!
Shoecumbers!
Goocumbers!
Moocumbers!
Newcumbers!
We're even stocking…
Poocumbers!
Bluecumbers!
Whocumbers!
Twocumbers!
Gluecumbers!
Screwcumbers!
Zoocumbers!
All fresh today!

Animal Talk

Dogs bark
Pigeons coo
Wolves howl
Cows moo
Snakes hiss
Crows caw
Cats purr
Lions roar
Ducks quack
Parrots squawk
I wonder what the animals say?
If only they could talk!

Have a Great Day!

Reach up high
Touch your toes
Waggle your fingers
Wiggle your nose
Spin on the spot
Stomp your feet
Shake your bottom
Clap the beat
Leap in the air
Shout 'Hooray!'
Wave to a buddy
Say 'Have a great day!'

Anywhere

Over mountains
In the sea
Down a dark hole
Up a tree
To a castle
Inside cars
Around a jungle
Beyond the stars
Through a wardrobe
Here and there
Books will take you anywhere

Swim with mermaids
Ride a rocket
Hide a dragon in your pocket
Dance with unicorns
Sing with whales
Tell a monster fairytales
Play with aliens
Hunt a bear
Books will take you anywhere

If you want fun, they're always there
Books will take you anywhere

HOW TO DRAW SUPER SLOTH!

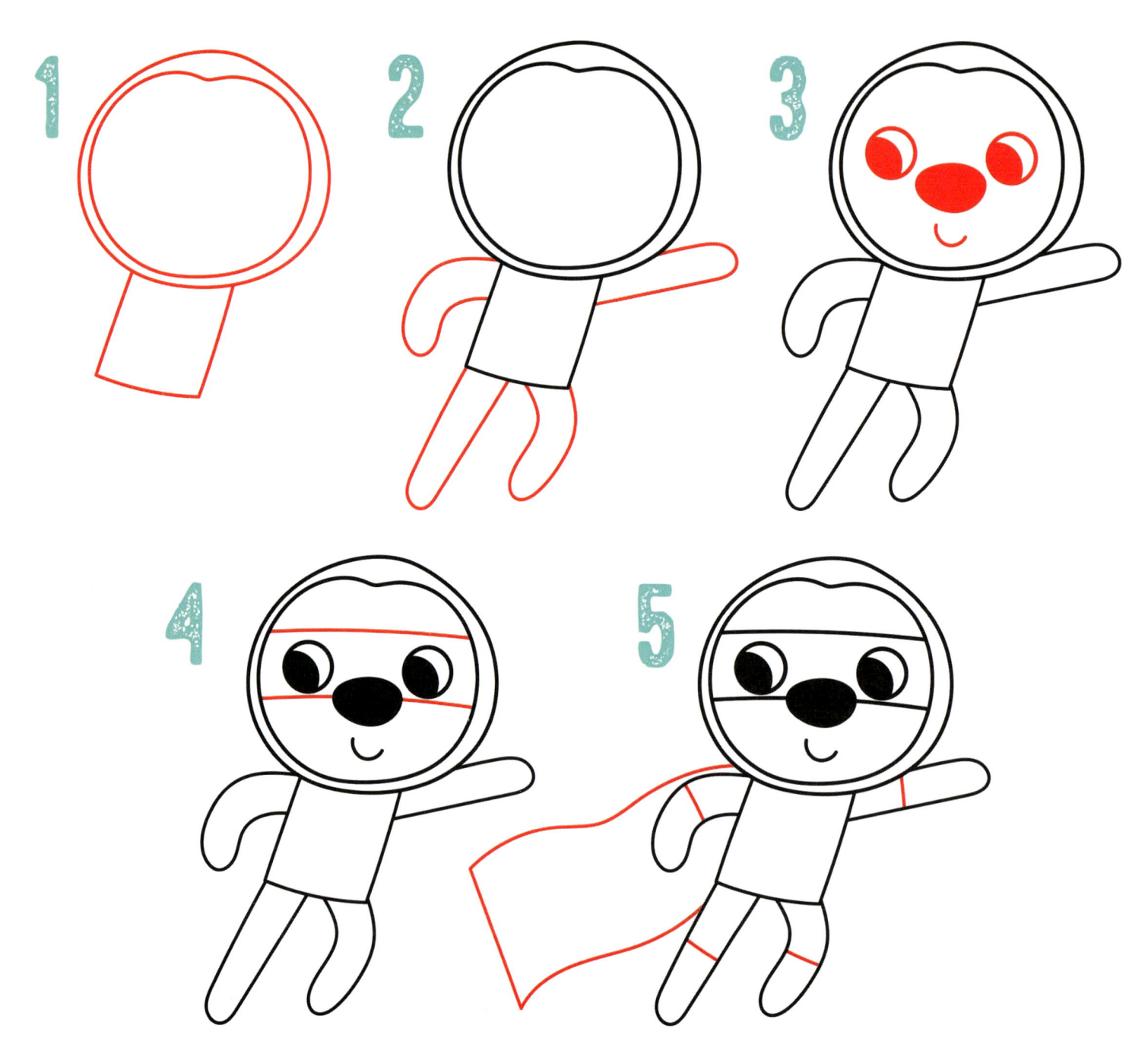

1.
2.
3.
4.
5.

Now use your imagination to add more detail to Super Sloth! What colour is their costume? Can you design them a logo? What about weapons or special powers?! Add your ideas to bring your character to life!

ABOUT THE AUTHOR

Kev is an author, illustrator and poet from Devon, UK.
He grew up with a love of books, comics and cartoons which inspired him to write and draw. Kev loves bringing ideas to life and, as a former primary school teacher, has a keen interest in educational ideas. His first book, 'B is for Blobfish', was inspired when planning a science lesson and features a wide range of unusual and unloved animals.

Kev can remember writing his first poem when he was 8 years old and loves poetry as it allows him to play with ideas.
He enjoys playing football and his favourite team is Norwich City.
Kev is also a town crier and Punch and Judy performer.

Kev is represented by Authors Abroad for school visits. For more information, visit:

https://www.authorsabroad.com/search-authors/kev-payne

As an author and illustrator, Kev is represented by Advocate Art. His clients include Scholastic, Ladybird, OUP and Crayola. His folio can be seen here:
https://www.advocate-art.com/kevin-payne

Kev used to look like this. Now he doesn't.

WWW.KEVPAYNE.COM

ALSO AVAILABLE

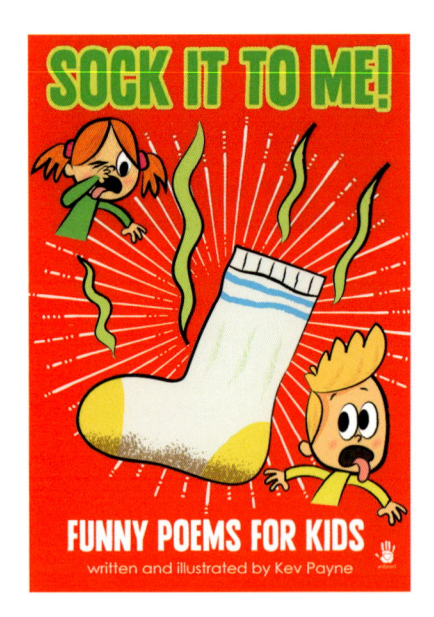

SOCK IT TO ME!

Have you ever covered a baby in ketchup? Have you had to sit on the naughty step? Have you got a magic bike? Have you ever swallowed a fly?! Poet, illustrator and teacher, Kev Payne, has. Join him as he presents a collection of over 50 poems about sausages, school, science, balloons, long car journeys and exactly what teachers are thinking when they are stood up at the front.

"A laugh-out-loud extravaganza of poetry for children!"
Dan Metcalf, Author of Codebusters, The Lottie Lipton Adventures, Jamie Jones and Dino Wars.

'B' IS FOR BLOBFISH

Think you know your A, B, C?
Take a unique journey around the animal kingdom meeting creatures that are often overlooked and under-loved.

Which animal likes to take sand baths?
Which has a pot belly to help digest leaves?
Which creature has tentacles for a nose?
Find out the answers to these, and more, in 'B is for Blobfish'!

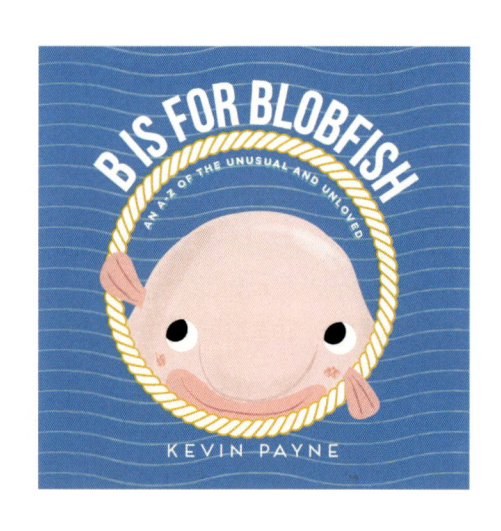

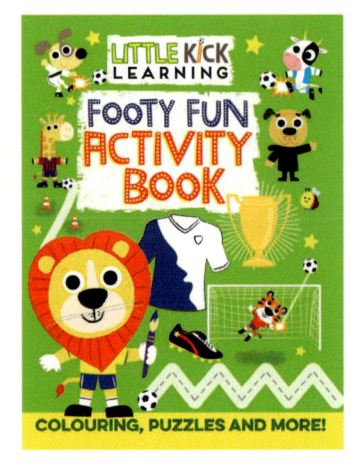

FOOTY FUN ACTIVITY BOOK

Are you ready for some footy fun?!

This activity book has kit designing, colouring, word tracing and more to keep your kids entertained.

For children aged 3-7, this football activity book is perfect for young learners and footy fans!

Find out more about books Kev has written and illustrated at

WWW.KEVPAYNE.COM